The Girls' Guide to
ZOMBIES

Everything Vital about
These Undead Monsters

Jen Jones

® **www.raintreepublishers.co.uk**
Visit our website to find out
more information about
Raintree books.

To order:
☎ Phone 0845 6044371
🖷 Fax +44 (0) 1865 312263
🖳 Email myorders@raintreepublishers.co.uk

Customers from outside the UK please telephone +44 1865 312262

Raintree is an imprint of Capstone Global
Library Limited, a company incorporated in
England and Wales having its registered office
at 7 Pilgrim Street, London, EC4V 6LB
– Registered company number: 6695582

First published by Capstone Press, a
Capstone imprint in 2011
First published in the United Kingdom in
paperback in 2012
The moral rights of the proprietor have
been asserted.

Edited by Kathryn Clay and Laura Knowles
Designed by Tracy Davies
Media research by Marcie Spence
Originated by Capstone Global Library Ltd
Printed and bound in China by South China
Printing Company Ltd

ISBN 978 1 406 24244 7 (paperback)
16 15 14 13 12
10 9 8 7 6 5 4 3 2 1

**British Library Cataloguing in
Publication Data**
Jones, Jen.
Zombies. -- (Girls' guide to everything
unexplained)
398.4'5-dc23
A full catalogue record for this book is
available from the British Library.

Acknowledgements
We would like to thank the following for
permission to reproduce photographs: 123RF:
Francesco Carta, 27 (bottom); Alamy Images:
Mary Evans Picture Library, 15; AP Images:
Alastair Grant, 9 (top); Capstone Press, 29
(both); Getty Images, Inc.: Adhil Rangel/
LatinContent, 25 (top), Gareth Cattermole, 25
(bottom), Keith Leman/WireImage, 9 (bottom),
Matt Carr, 28 (top); iStockphoto: antonbrand,
cover, (illustrated hand), diane39, cover (hand),
22, Floriana, cover (smoke), ianmcdonnell, 23
(top), ninjaprints, 7, 11, SochAnam, 17 (middle),
26, wwing, 27 (middle); Newscom: 5, Market
Square Productions, 12 (right), United Artists,
12 (left), Vaughan Stephen/SIPA, 23 (bottom),
28 (bottom); Shutterstock: Bliznetsov, 16, 18,
Dmitrijs Dmitrijevs, 17 (top), Mopic, 27 (top),
OnFocus, cover (girl), S.M., 17 (bottom),
TomaszBidermann, 23 (middle).

Every effort has been made to contact copyright
holders of any material reproduced in this book.
Any omissions will be rectified in subsequent
printings if notice is given to the publisher.

Disclaimer
All the internet addresses (URLs) given in this
book were valid at the time of going to press.
However, due to the dynamic nature of the
internet, some addresses may have changed, or
sites may have changed or ceased to exist since
publication. While the author and publisher
regret any inconvenience this may cause readers,
no responsibility for any such changes can be
accepted by either the author or the publisher.

Contents

Some words are shown in **bold**, like this. You can find out what they mean by looking in the word bar at the bottom of the page, or in the glossary.

Chapter 1

If I only had a brain …

In Michael Jackson's "Thriller" music video, **corpses** rise from the grave to dance and sing. In *Night of the Living Dead*, flesh-eating ghouls search out tasty human treats. What do these creepy creatures have in common? They're zombies, of course!

Most zombies are dead creatures that rise from their graves to terrify the living. Other zombies are created from a virus or by a bite that makes them go into a **trance**. No matter how they form, zombies share a common goal – to feast on human brains! Grey matter is all that matters to these scary creatures.

corpse: dead body

But take another look at these living dead. They may have peeling flesh and missing limbs, but make no mistake...

Zombies are quickly approaching star-status among the living.

Be it in books or on the big screen, zombies are more popular than ever. Read on to get the low-down on these crusty creatures.

Night of the Living Dead, 1968

trance: awake state where you are not really aware of what is happening around you

WHAT'S IN A NAME?

The word zombie is said to come from the words *jumbie* and *nzambi*. Jumbie means "ghost" in West Indian. Nzambi is an African word meaning "soul of a dead person". Some Chinese legends describe zombie vampires called *Kuang Shi*. Unlike regular zombies, Kuang Shi don't moan or have bodies that are falling apart. Instead, they act as soldiers who mindlessly follow orders.

So how do the dead rise again as zombies?

There's more than one answer to that question. Many believe zombies rise from the grave after being **revived** by a sorcerer's curse. The sorcerer becomes the zombies' master and controls their actions – for good or evil.

It's a different story for zombies created by viruses or other causes. "Zombie viruses" attack the brains of normal people. The victims instantly develop a craving for human flesh, especially brains. Like vampires, zombies can increase their numbers with one bite to an unsuspecting victim.

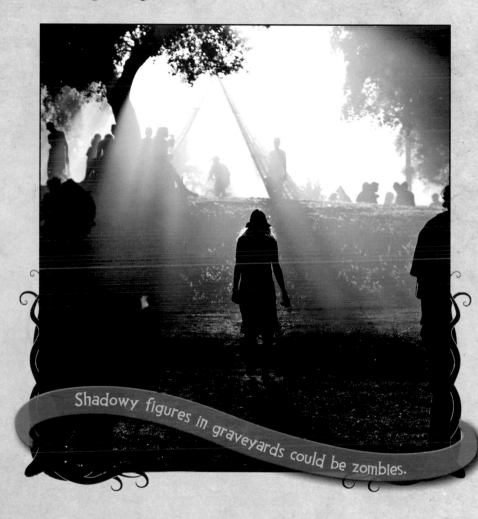

Shadowy figures in graveyards could be zombies.

revive: bring someone back to life

ON THE PAGE AND ON SCREEN

Zombie stories have been around for decades, but they have become more popular in recent years. Zombies now share the spotlight with vampires, werewolves, and wizards. And it's easy to see why. Zombies are fun to read about and even more fun to watch on screen!

Need some inspiration for spotting zombies?

Look no further than Aaron Starmer's *Dweeb: Burgers, Beasts, and Brainwashed Bullies*. In this book, five brainy school kids are stuck in the school's basement. Their mission is to work out why their school has suddenly gone haywire. Greasy fast food is being served in the canteen. Bullies are suddenly super-sweet. And zombies are walking the halls. This mystery can only be solved by Denton, Wendell, Eddie, Elijah, and Bijay – D.W.E.E.B!

Classic zombies

Best-selling books such as *Pride and Prejudice and Zombies* are putting a zombie twist on classic novels. Zombies are also cropping up in other classic tales, including *The Wizard of Oz* and *Huckleberry Finn*. Zombies are truly becoming stars of the page.

Pride and Prejudice and Zombies

Pathogen

Pathogen isn't cool just because it focuses on zombies. This horror flick is also the first-ever feature film made by an American teenager. Emily Hagins wrote and directed the film when she was just 12 years old. The film features a young girl named Dannie. Dannie must save her town from widespread zombie attacks. *Zombie Girl: The Movie* is a **documentary** about the making of this film.

Emily Hagins

documentary: film or TV programme about real situations and people

Chapter 2
A to Z zombie history

The rise of zombies

Compared to the long history of vampires and werewolves, zombies are somewhat new on the **supernatural** scene. Many zombie legends began in Haiti, a small country in the Caribbean. In the early 1900s, Haitian people shared stories of powerful masters called *bokors*. Haitians believed that bokors could create mindless slaves.

supernatural: something that cannot be given an ordinary explanation

Bokors used black magic and "zombie powder" to make the living become the undead. The zombie powder mix included ingredients such as marine toads, plants, and puffer fish. Puffer fish are extremely poisonous. Eating the wrong part of this fish can cause someone to become numb or even paralyzed. A deadly mix, indeed!

Stories say that these undead could hear, speak, move, and eat. Their master treated these zombies as slaves. But these poor undead had no idea of their zombie state. Their brains and memories were mush.

Zombies roam the night.

ZOMBIES IN AMERICA

In 1929, William Seabrook wrote a book called *The Magic Island* about his travels to Haiti. The book described mindless zombie slaves working in sugarcane fields. *Time* magazine later credited Seabrook as the first person to introduce the word zombie to Americans.

Books and films made zombies popular.

A few years earlier, zombie-like characters played starring roles in pop culture. In 1922 writer H. P. Lovecraft wrote a short story called "Herbert West – Reanimator". The tale was one of the first to show the living dead as hungry, violent creatures.

In 1932, the movie *White Zombie* starred Bela Lugosi as a Haitian **hypnotist**. Even Disney got in on the action with a comic strip featuring "Bombie the Zombie" in 1949. Another important project in zombie history was 1968's *Night of the Living Dead*. In this classic film, gangs of hungry undead attack a small Pennsylvania town in the United States. The word "zombie" is never actually said in the film. But many people agree it's the most famous zombie flick of all time.

Since the 1980s, zombie films have become more popular than ever.

Hundreds of zombie films have been made. But most of them are too gory for young audiences. You may need to be over 15 or 18 years old to see them.

hypnotist: someone who puts people into a sleep-like state

THE REAL DEAL

It's hard to say if zombies are just a creation of Haitians and Hollywood.

 Over the years, many people have claimed they were zombies.

Others claim they have seen real-life zombies walking about. One of the most popular tales is of Clairvius Narcisse. He died in 1962. Some believe he was brought back to life and turned into a zombie. More than 200 people claimed to have spotted Clairvius wandering around after his death. Even his sister claimed she saw him! Another reported zombie was Felicia Felix-Mentor. She died in 1907, but people say they saw her walking around Haiti in the 1930s.

Inspired by such stories, a scientist named Wade Davis went to Haiti in 1982. He studied how people might become zombies. He sent "zombie potions" to science labs. Scientists found that the potions made rats act like they were in a trance. From mice to men, it seems zombies just might be the real deal!

Clairvius Narcisse

Chapter 3

Spotting zombies

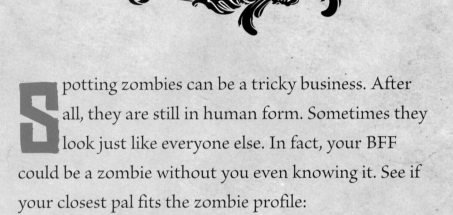

Spotting zombies can be a tricky business. After all, they are still in human form. Sometimes they look just like everyone else. In fact, your BFF could be a zombie without you even knowing it. See if your closest pal fits the zombie profile:

Best friend or zombie?

Discoloured, pale skin: Life after death isn't pretty! Most zombies' skin looks blue or green because their blood is no longer pumping. Their skin might even be rotting or have dried bloody patches on it.

 ZOMBIE ALERT: Does your BFF always carry a compact so she can powder her face? She might be trying to hide a crusty complexion!

Blank expression: Zombies tend to be a blank slate. Their faces show zero signs of emotion. With glassy eyes and open mouths, zombies look like they are sleepwalking.

ZOMBIE ALERT: Does your BFF spend most of her time daydreaming? There might be a reason she always seems to be in outer space.

Missing limbs: Missing an arm? No problem. Lacking a leg? No sweat. One of the perks of being dead is that zombies are forever numb. So losing a limb is no big deal.

ZOMBIE ALERT: Is your BFF's closet full of long, flowing dresses? Maybe she's just into the boho look. Or maybe she's hiding a lost limb!

ZOMBIE RUNDOWN

Now that you're a pro at spotting zombies, it's time to kick it up a notch. There are many kinds of zombies, so it's important to know the difference. After all, if your BFF really is a zombie, you'll want to know what type you're facing! Here are the most common zombie types:

Voodoo zombie? You decide.

Voodoo *zombies* have been put under a spell by a mystery drug or powder. They become lifeless with no free will.

Philosophical *zombies*, also known as P-zombies, are undercover zombies. They look and act just like normal humans. Yet they have no soul or ability to think.

Hollywood zombies are the scariest of the bunch! These are the undead you have come to know and love on the big screen.

 These rotting zombies are always on the hunt for tasty human brains.

voodoo: religion that began in Africa and is practised in Haiti

philosophical: relating to the search for wisdom

QUIZ: Which type of zombie are you?

It's not just your BFF who may be a zombie. You could also have common features of the undead. But what zombie style fits you the best? Take the quiz below to find out.

Your teacher is giving a maths lesson. You find yourself:

a) dozing off. None of the info ever seems to sink in!

b) wanting to call her "Master".

c) wondering if her brain is tasty.

d) taking notes and listening. Algebra is so cool!

You're sealing envelopes for your upcoming party, and you get a paper cut. What's your reaction?

a) No biggie. Can you pass the stamps?

b) That's nothing. I'm used to pain.

c) I did? I didn't feel anything.

d) Ouch! Where are the bandages?

Your dream job would be:

a) couch potato

b) personal assistant

c) brain surgeon

d) anything that involves one of your passions

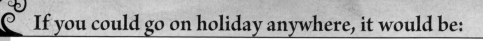

If you could go on holiday anywhere, it would be:

a) Australia – everyone there is so laid-back!

b) Haiti

c) Hungary, because you're always hungry!

d) Portugal, for its beauty and beaches.

What's your favourite kind of make-up?

a) I don't wear make-up because it covers my blue skin.

b) powder in a compact – and lots of it!

c) white face paint and fake blood!

d) strawberry lip gloss

What's your IQ? (Trick question)

a) zero

b) zero

c) zero

d) more than zero!

Look through your answers to find out which zombie group is your best fit. If you circled:

Mostly As: You might look human, but you're really a P-zombie.

Mostly Bs: You would be most at home among voodoo zombies.

Mostly Cs: Hello La-la-land! You're a Hollywood zombie all the way.

Mostly Ds: No doubt about it, you're human as can be.

✣ ✣ ✣ ✣ ✣ ✣ ✣ ✣ ✣ ✣ ✣ ✣ ✣ ✣ ✣ ✣ ✣ ✣

Chapter 4

Zombie strengths and weaknesses

Wanted dead or alive: zombie strengths

No matter what kind of zombie you meet, you will probably have a tough fight on your hands. Zombies may not be brainy, but they are determined to find brains. To become successful searchers, they've developed some super strengths.

Zombies are dead but strong.

Strength in numbers: Zombies tend to travel in groups. Together they can invade an area and attack nearby humans. Zombie experts even warn of the undead taking over the world. In *Harry Potter and the Half-Blood Prince,* a sea of zombies rises from the lake to guard Voldemort's treasure.

No pain, all gain: Imagine scraping your knee or cutting your finger. Though it might be painful to you, a zombie would barely blink an eye. Because they are already dead, zombies don't experience pain. It's not unusual to see a zombie with a knife in its shoulder or a bloody forehead.

Power plus: Zombies may not move fast, but they are super-strong. They can tear off a victim's limbs or break through windows and walls. The "Thriller" music video is a great example. Zombies smash through the floors and windows to get to Michael Jackson's date.

WALK LIKE A ZOMBIE

The new trend of "zombie walks" further blurs the line between fact and fantasy. Imagine hundreds of zombies walking the streets of your town or invading the shopping centre. Thanks to zombie walks, it could actually happen. These public events gather large groups of zombie fans to honour the undead. The biggest zombie walk ever was in Ledbury, Herefordshire, in 2009. More than 4,000 people showed up for the world's largest zombie gathering.

But you don't have to be undead to join in a zombie parade. All you need is a little make-up and a few friends. It can be as simple as a walk around your neighbourhood. If you want to go big, you can start a public gathering in your town. Check out Internet sites for ideas and upcoming walks in your area. And don't forget to dress the part. A pale white face, dark eye circles, fake blood, and torn clothes make the perfect zombie look.

Zombies out on the town

Zombie walks are a hot trend.

Undoing the undead: zombie weaknesses

How do you kill something that is already dead? For zombie hunters, that's the million-pound question. Zombies can't feel anything, so the usual weapons won't work. Yet it's not impossible to stop a zombie in its tracks.

Off with its head: The only way to kill a zombie for good is to knock off its noggin. After all, a zombie can't think about brains if it doesn't have one! Of course, zombies aren't very smart in the first place, making it easy to outwit them.

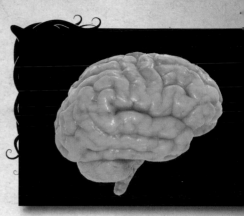

Shake things up: For those who squirm at the thought of knocking off zombie heads, here's a cleaner approach. Smelling salts are used to awaken people who faint. Regular salt can do the same thing for zombies. Haitians believe that giving a zombie salt will bring it back to its senses. After the zombie eats salt, it will often go back to its grave and die for good. Just ask the witches in the Disney flick *Hocus Pocus*. They spread a circle of salt to keep zombies away.

Go the distance: Unlike lightning-quick vampires and werewolves, most zombies move like snails. They walk stiffly with their arms out in front of them. So if you find yourself being chased by a zombie, it shouldn't be too hard to outrun it. In the spooky cartoon "Dial 'Z' for Zombie", the Simpson clan manages to do just that. Bart accidentally casts a spell that awakens a whole cemetery. But Bart and Lisa are too quick to let the zombies catch them.

ZOMBIE AWARDS

Most Frightful Filmmaker
Emily Hagins (*Pathogen*)

She already has one film under her belt. Who knows what else is in store for this young star?

Coolest Zombie Moves
The cast of "Thriller"

Zombies that rise from the grave to sing and dance with Michael Jackson? There's a reason this 14-minute video has been called the greatest music video ever.

Most Daring Zombie-Hunters
Elizabeth Bennet and Mr Darcy
(Pride and Prejudice and Zombies)

Whether hunting zombies or romancing each other, this pair can't be beat.

Best Theme Song
"Zombie" by the Cranberries

Few zombies can resist a song that repeats their name over and over.

Cutest Couple
Toffee and Jonny
(Zombie Prom)

Even turning into a zombie won't stop Jonny from taking Toffee to the prom in this zombie musical.

GLOSSARY

corpse dead body

documentary film or TV programme about real situations and people

hypnotist someone who puts people into a sleep-like state

philosophical relating to the search for wisdom

revive bring someone back to life

supernatural something that cannot be given an ordinary explanation

trance conscious state where you are not really aware of what is happening around you

voodoo religion that began in Africa and is practised in Haiti

FIND OUT MORE

Encyclopedia Horrifica: The Terrifying Truth about Vampires, Ghosts, Monsters, and More, Joshua Gee (Scholastic, 2007)

How to Be a Zombie: The Essential Guide for Anyone Who Craves Brains, Serena Valentino (Candlewick Press, 2010)

The Undead, Jim Pipe (TickTock Books, 2008)

Vampires and the Undead (The Dark Side), Anita Ganeri (Wayland, 2010)

Zombies on the Loose (Clash), Anne Rooney (TickTock Books, 2008)

INDEX